May God's Love Be With
You and Bring you Back
To Visit N.C. often -
1997   The Edwards'

NORTH CAROLINA
An Intimate View

The Intimate Bookshop

CLB 1593
This 1990 edition published by The Intimate Bookshop,
by arrangement with Outlet Book Company, Inc, a Random House Company,
225 Park Avenue South, New York, New York 10003.
© 1986 Colour Library Books Ltd, Godalming, Surrey, England.
All rights reserved.
Printed and bound in Hong Kong.
ISBN 0 517 62355 2
8 7 6 5 4 3 2 1

Introduction

My brother, Wallace, and I used to walk through the woods of Mecklenburg County, following the rabbit paths, to a great outcropping of granite boulders hidden by tall pines – a cool, dark and primeval setting we called "the secret place." We imagined we were the first ever to set foot there.

There's a street there today, with curbs, sidewalks and fire hydrants. The boulders have become an attractive feature in somebody's back yard. They've paved the rabbit paths, and our secret place has become public.

It's hard to keep secret the sort of evocative beauty contained by North Carolina. The Indians thought they were the only ones who knew about it, but a mariner sailing for England, after one glance, sent back word to Queen Elizabeth I that he had found the "goodliest land under the cope of heaven." After that first example of real estate promotion, visitors have been coming from afar to see for themselves. Many of them, being charmed, never leave. Six million people call themselves "Tar Heels" today, nearly twice as many as in the days when my brother and I explored the forest around our home.

But abundant natural beauty remains, as this book gives evidence. Every morning, as the sun comes up on the barrier islands of the outer banks, the gulls still swoop and call above the ocean breakers; every night, as the sun sets in the mountains, the mist still hangs low along the streams; the native dogwoods still put on their glorious show every April, and the ancient oaks set October ablaze. And one of North Carolina's enduring satisfactions is that even her largest cities are not so large as to prevent a pavement-weary urbanite from finding solace in the countryside in a drive of half an hour.

Think of this "intimate view" of North Carolina as an index to some of the beautiful sights of one of the most beautiful states. Then, if you can, with this book under your arm, venture out along the byways. Somewhere – among the nodding sea oats at the margin of the land, along a green fairway in the Sand Hills, in a historic village of the rolling Piedmont, or beside a crystal river in a hollow of the Blue Ridge – you may find a secret place to call your own.

CHARLES KURALT

Facing page: the Old Well at the University of North Carolina, Chapel Hill.

Left: the splendid State Capitol amid its six acres of wooded grounds in Raleigh (these pages). Above: the Legislative Building, (above center) the Coliseum and State Fairgrounds, site of the annual State Fair (top).

Named after Sir Walter Raleigh, North Carolina's capital city (these pages) was laid out in 1792 by William Christmas. The original plan involved five public greens, and today Raleigh boasts over three hundred parks, plazas and gardens. Above: a tranquil waterway in Pullen Park, (right) an aerial view of St. Mary's College, and (below) the Legislative Building, which was designed by Edward Durell Stone, the architect of the John F. Kennedy Center for the Performing Arts in Washington D.C.

Built between 1883 and 1891, the Governor's Mansion (left) in Raleigh (these pages), with its numerous gables, ornately carved verandahs and patterned roof, is considered to be one of the country's finest examples of "gingerbread" Victorian architecture. The majestic State Capitol (above) was built between 1833 and 1840 in the Greek Revival Doric style. Two miles to the west is situated the North Carolina State University, with its imposing Clock Tower (top).

Facing page: Concord United Methodist Church, and (bottom) the town of Chapel Hill. Now a major manufacturing center, Durham (remaining pictures) owes much of its growth to the Duke family's tobacco industry, which flourished after the Civil War. Left: a house in Trinity Park, (bottom left) the Duke Chapel, on Duke University's West Campus, and (below) the Duke homestead.

Facing page: (top) Duke University Hospital and (bottom) the Sarah B. Duke Gardens, both in Durham. Right: the famous Playmakers Theatre and (above) the Old Well, at the University of North Carolina, and (top) Morehead Planetarium, all in Chapel Hill. Above right: Guilford College, in Greensboro.

Top: the Chapel of the Cross, and (right)
the Bell Tower of the University of North
Carolina, both at Chapel Hill (facing
page). Above: Guilford Courthouse National
Military Park, northwest of Greensboro.

Old East (above and top), at the University of
North Carolina in Chapel Hill, is both the
university's and the town's oldest building.
Completed in 1795, it has been beautifully
preserved in its simple, Colonial style and
is still in full use today. Right: the campus
of Duke University, Durham. Facing page:
(top) a magnolia bloom, and (bottom) Nash-
Hooper House, which was built in 1772 by the
Revolutionary War hero General Francis Nash,
in the historic town of Hillsborough.

Top: the Smith Reynolds Library at Wake Forest University, in Winston-Salem. Only five blocks away from this busy city's financial district is Old Salem, an 18th-century Moravian town with many beautifully-restored buildings, including the Home Moravian Church (right) and the houses on Main Street (above).

Among the many attractions of Old Salem are Salem Academy and College, with its elegant Howard Mondthaler Science Building (right), and Reynolda House (top), with its surrounding village and farm. This model, self-supporting settlement was constructed in 1917 by the namesake and founder of the R.J. Reynolds Tobacco Company. Furnished in a variety of international styles, the superb mansion also contains a comprehensive collection of American paintings.

Above: a bluegrass fiddler at Mount Airy, near the border with Virginia. Top: the 600-foot-high, granite dome of Stone Mountain State Park, near Roaring Gap. The scenic Blue Ridge Parkway follows the backbone of the southern Appalachians for 469 miles and is lined by many intriguing and beautiful sights, including 6,000-acre Doughton Park (overleaf right), site of Brinegar Cabin (right), where the Brinegar family wove cloth between 1885 and 1935. Overleaf: (top left) the Green Park Inn at Blowing Rock, one of the oldest resorts in the southern Appalachians, and (bottom left) Grandfather Mountain, in the Blue Ridge range north of Linville.

Above: the Thomas Wolfe Memorial, childhood home of the famous novelist, and (top) Grove Park Inn, a distinctive resort built in 1913 on the slopes of Beaucatcher Mountain, both in Asheville. Situated along the Blue Ridge Parkway near Blowing Rock is the Moses Cone Memorial Park, with its sumptuous manor house (left). The park was once the 3,500-acre estate of Moses H. Cone, who, by founding the Cone Mills, initiated the development of the southern textile industry. Overleaf: Hanging Rock (right), in 4,040-acre Hanging Rock State Park, affords breathtaking views of the forests around Danbury. The colorful sport of hot air ballooning (left) also provides an aerial perspective on the state.

Above: Connemara Farm at Flat Rock, the home of poet Carl Sandburg. Biltmore House and Gardens (remaining pictures), in Asheville, were built in 1895 by George Vanderbilt. The 225-room manor house (left) is considered to be one of the most opulent homes in the world.

Top: a flag flies above the awesome, 225-foot-high Chimney Rock, in
Chimney Rock Park, (above) a wooden house in the depths of rugged
Pisgah National Forest, and (right and overleaf) views from the
Blue Ridge Parkway of the spectacular Great Smoky Mountains.

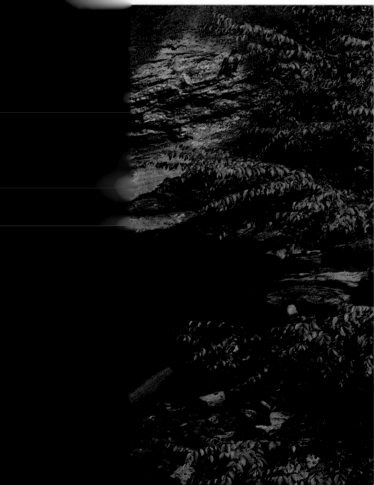

Left: a waterfall in Pisgah National Forest, (top) Looking Glass Creek spilling over smooth Sliding Rock, and (above) a Cherokee at the Oconaluftee Indian Village. Overleaf: (top right) Mingus Mill, (bottom right) foothills near the Maggie Valley, and (left) rich farmland in the Great Smoky Mountains.

Previous pages: a view from Newfound Gap Road, part of the North Carolina-Tennessee line through the Great Smoky Mountains. Left: a house in the Myers Park area, (above) the home of Hezekiah Alexander, (facing page top) Queens College, and (facing page bottom) Kuralt House, all in Charlotte. Top: the James K. Polk Birthplace Memorial in Pineville.

Top: the birthplace of President Andrew Johnson, at Mordecai Historic Park in Raleigh. Charlotte (remaining pictures), once a Confederate naval base, is now a busy, modern center of trade and industry. Above: the Mint Museum of Art, which was formerly a branch of the U.S. Mint, (top far left) the Charlotte Motor Speedway, (far left) a view from James B. Marshall Park, (left) buildings on Trade Street, (above left) Mecklenburg County Courthouse, and (top left) the modern Convention Center, with the Radisson Plaza Hotel beyond.

Top: one of over two dozen golf courses around Pinehurst, the state's golfing mecca. Above and right: military exercises, and (facing page) a memorial, at Fort Bragg, Fayetteville, a training center for airborne troops.

Among a wealth of historic sights in Wilmington (previous pages) are Poplar Grove Plantation (right), the Governor Dudley Mansion (top left) of 1825, and the *USS North Carolina* (bottom left) opposite downtown Wilmington, on the Cape Fear River. Below: Caswell Beach Lighthouse, and (remaining pictures) Southport, both at Cape Fear.

Fort Macon (left), built in 1834 as a coastal defence work, is a fine example of early-19th-century fortification. Top: a waterfront home in historic New Bern (above), which was North Carolina's first capital city. Its state capitol, Tryon Palace (overleaf), was built in 1770 and considered in its day to be America's finest building. (Top left) museum staff at the palace, (bottom left) the dining room, and (right) the 18th-century English-style Maude Moore Latham Memorial Garden.

Above: a ferry boat at Minnesott, one of many small fishing towns along the low-lying coast of Pamlico County. Anchored off the coast of Manteo, one of the main towns on Roanoke Island, is the *Elizabeth II* (left and top), a 69-foot-long replica of the type of bark which brought colonists to the island during the 16th century. Overleaf: Manteo, with (top right) Dare County Courthouse, and (center right) a scene from a performance at the Lost Colony Theater (bottom right) re-enacting the mysterious disappearence of Raleigh's Roanoke colony in the 1580s. Also in remembrance of the brave men and women of the colony were planted the Elizabethan Gardens, at the center of which lies the fine Sunken Garden (left).

In 1903, from the sand banks by Kill Devil Hill, Wilbur and
Orville Wright flew the first passenger-carrying, heavier-than-air
flying machine. On the same site today, a replica of this plane,
the *Kittyhawk* (below), can be seen at the Wright Brothers National
Memorial, one of the many attractions of Cape Hatteras National
Seashore. Bottom: the "Ghost Ship", and (inset left) the sand
dunes of Jockey's Ridge, both at Nags Head, which allegedly
derives its name from the early residents' habit of tying lanterns
about their horses' necks, taking them down to the dunes on stormy
nights and luring merchant ships aground in order to salvage their
cargo. The tallest light on the American coast, the distinctive,
spiral-patterned Cape Hatteras Lighthouse (left) is 198 feet high
and was built in 1870 to warn vessels of the Diamond Shoals, the
sand bars off this beautiful but treacherous seashore.

Top: a grand home in Elizabeth City near Albemarle Sound, which is sheltered by the Outer Banks (remaining pictures). Above: catamarans at Nags Head, (right) Bodie Island Lighthouse, and (overleaf) the 60-foot, granite Wright Monument Shaft, at the Wright Brothers National Memorial.